Exploring Space

Written by Mary-Anne Creasy

Flying Start
to Literacy®

Contents

Introduction

Hundreds of years ago, rulers in Europe were hungry for gold, spices and faster sea routes. They sent **navigators** and explorers out in small wooden ships to find the "New World".

These navigators and explorers sailed into the vast unknown ocean. Many feared that they might sail over the edge of the ocean because they thought the earth was flat. They had nothing to guide them but myths, stories and incomplete or incorrect maps. Ships had to carry all their supplies, but they didn't know how long the food and water would need to last. Many sailors feared pirates, sea monsters, disease and death.

A sailor used this tool called a cross-staff. It was used to measure the angle between the horizon and a star. By knowing this angle, sailors could work out their location.

Wooden sailing ships in the harbour
in Lisbon, Portugal, about 400 years ago

The explorers and their crew were often gone for years,
some returning with wealth, glory and incredible stories
of their discoveries. Others never returned.

Now, this same human spirit drives us to explore another
unknown world – space and what lies beyond. These
brave new explorers also face many dangers, including
the uncertainty of whether they will return.

The journey into space

When our journey into space first began 70 years ago, it enthralled the world – this was humanity's newest adventure.

NASA launched its first spacecraft on 11 October, 1958.

The space race

Both the United States of America and the Soviet Union developed space technology at the same time, around 70 years ago. The Soviets launched the first **satellite** in 1957. The Americans did not want the Soviets to control space, so they created the National Aeronautics and Space Administration (NASA) and launched the first American spacecraft in 1958. This started the "space race".

By the early 1960s, both the Americans and the Soviets had successfully orbited the earth. But the American president, John F. Kennedy, wanted the United States to achieve a milestone in the space race – to put the first human on the moon.

It was going to cost billions of dollars, and well over half of all Americans opposed the idea of putting a man on the moon. At that time, one-fifth of American citizens did not have adequate food, clothing and shelter.

The Soviet Union

The Soviet Union was formed in 1922, when Russia and many neighbouring countries, such as Ukraine, Belarus and Latvia, joined together as one. In 1991, the Soviet Union was dissolved and each country reverted to its original name.

Aim for the moon

President Kennedy had to persuade the American public that putting a man on the moon would be the greatest scientific achievement in the history of the United States. In September 1962, President Kennedy gave a speech about how difficult this would be, but still worth the money and effort. The President vowed to reach the moon by the end of the decade and, in 1969, the United States blasted a rocket into space. The world watched in awe as two astronauts – Neil Armstrong and Buzz Aldrin – stepped out of their spacecraft and walked on the moon. They had done it: the Americans had won the race to the moon.

The United States flew five other manned missions to the moon between 1969 and 1972, and in total, 12 American astronauts have walked on the moon.

To this day, no one person has travelled further into space. But these courageous explorers proved that space was another New World and that there was more to discover.

Neil Armstrong and Buzz Aldrin plant the American flag on the moon, July 1969.

Those who came before us made certain that this country rode the first waves of the industrial revolutions, the first waves of modern inventions, and the first wave of nuclear power, and this generation does not intend to founder in the backwash of the coming age of space. We mean to be part of it and we mean to lead it . . .

We choose to go to the moon in this decade and do the other things, not because they are easy, but because they are hard, because that goal will serve to organise and measure the best of our energies and skills . . .

John F. Kennedy, September 1962

The technology that was developed during the space race and the creation of NASA has shown that Kennedy's statement has proved to be true:

> **Space exploration has been for the benefit of all humans.**

Many of the inventions that made space travel possible have made our lives on Earth better. Some of these inventions are even helping save lives.

The Skylab space station using a huge space blanket as a sun shield.

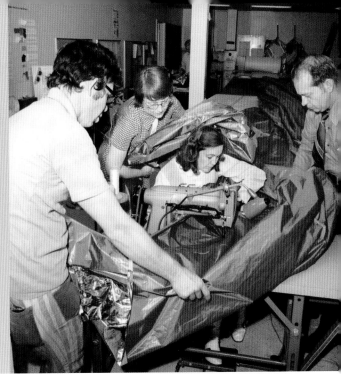

Making a sunscreen for the Skylab Orbital Workshop (OWS) at Johnson Space Center, Houston, Texas, May 1973

Space blankets

When NASA began the space program, it needed to protect spacecraft from the dangerous sunrays in space. The solution was an ultrathin sheet of plastic with a layer of vaporised aluminium, creating a light yet strong material.

That material became the well-known space blanket, which today is used all over the world as a protective cover to prevent the loss of body heat. Loss of body heat can be dangerous to humans, so the blankets are used in many first-aid and emergency situations, such as earthquakes.

Water purification system

People need to drink water to survive, but there is no constant supply of fresh water in space. NASA developed water purification systems so that astronauts could recycle and then reuse all moisture as safe drinking water.

The same double-filter technology can now be found inside water bottles used by hikers and others to turn water from lakes and rivers into pure drinking water.

Teflon-coated fibreglass fabric

NASA asked inventors to create a special fabric for space suits. The fabric had to protect the astronauts from fire, ultraviolet damage and other dangers they might encounter in space. Today, this incredibly strong material is used to shelter parks, swimming pools and sports stadiums all over the world.

Smartphone-camera technology

Did you know that the cameras in our phones use technology developed by NASA? Scientists working for NASA developed digital image **sensors** to be smaller and require less power for use on spacecraft. These image sensors revolutionised cameras, allowing them to get smaller and smaller, and now we can take high-quality photos everywhere we go with our smartphones.

Athletic shoes

NASA scientists designed a shock-absorbent rubber moulding for astronauts' helmets. This rubber moulding inspired what is now a common feature in the soles of many athletic shoes.

The **satellite** is one of the greatest inventions of space travel. Satellites are launched into space by a rocket and orbit Earth. They contain a power source such as a battery, a computer and **antennae** that send signals back to Earth. Many satellites also have cameras that take photos and videos.

Satellites can be as small as a lunch box or as big as a school bus. When satellites are no longer active, they either move into an outer orbit or, if they are small, they just fall and burn up on entering Earth's atmosphere.

Did you know?
Space probes are robotic spacecraft that orbit or explore other planets, asteroids, the moon or even further out on the edge of our **solar system.** These probes transmit information back to scientists on Earth.

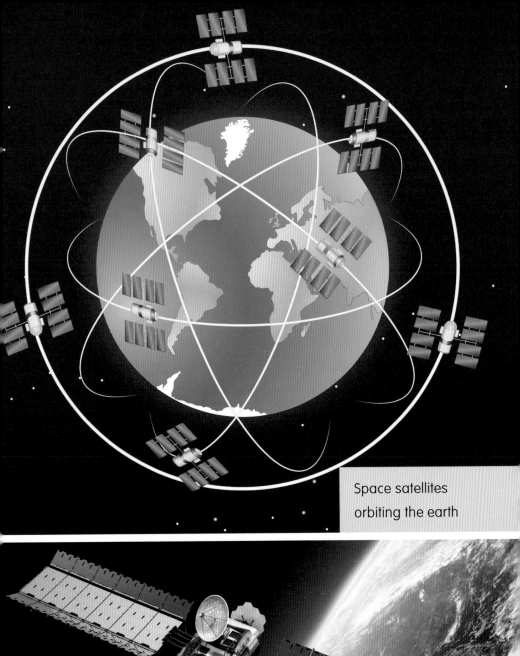

Space satellites
orbiting the earth

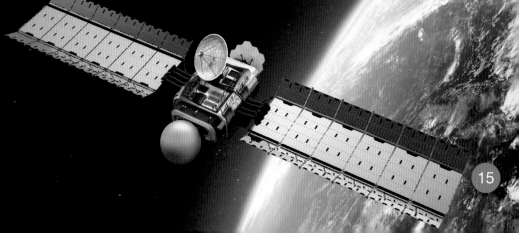

A communications satellite orbiting the earth

Communications satellites

Can't get cable TV? Just get a **satellite dish** and watch TV, listen to the radio or communicate on the move. A satellite dish is a powerful antenna that receives signals from the satellites orbiting the earth.

We use satellites for many things like TV, radio and telephones. Satellites for communication don't rely on a nearby phone tower or cable; they can transmit from anywhere.

A signal is transmitted from a ground station to a satellite and then back to another ground station

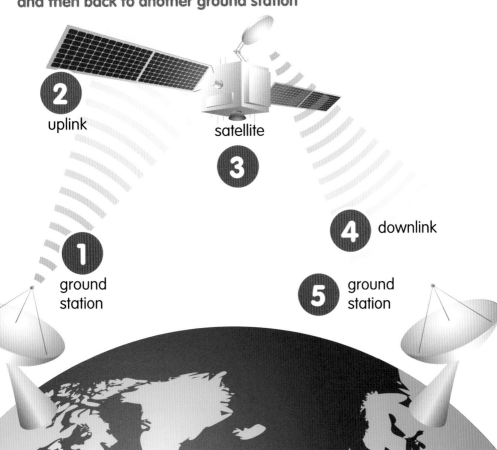

2 uplink

satellite

3

4 downlink

1 ground station

5 ground station

Global Positioning System (GPS)

Satellites can locate and track objects and people using mobile phone signals. We use this technology when we navigate in our cars with apps like Google Maps. We even use this technology when we play mobile games such as Pokémon Go.

Satellites are also vital in the rescue of sailors, hikers and anyone in difficulty in a remote area. If you have an emergency beacon or device, it can be switched on and the signal is sent to a satellite, which alerts rescue teams.

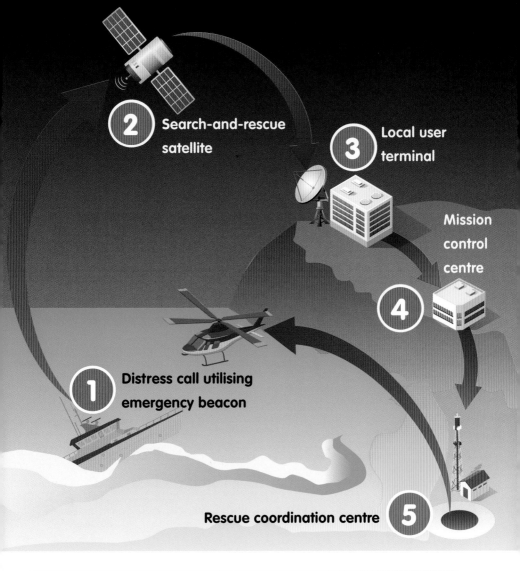

2 Search-and-rescue satellite

3 Local user terminal

Mission control centre

4

1 Distress call utilising emergency beacon

Rescue coordination centre **5**

Did you know?

In February 2018, a sailboat caught fire at sea. It could have ended in disaster for the crew, but a satellite picked up the distress signal from its emergency beacon. The US Air Force and Coast Guard were given the exact location of the boat from the signal and the crew was rescued.

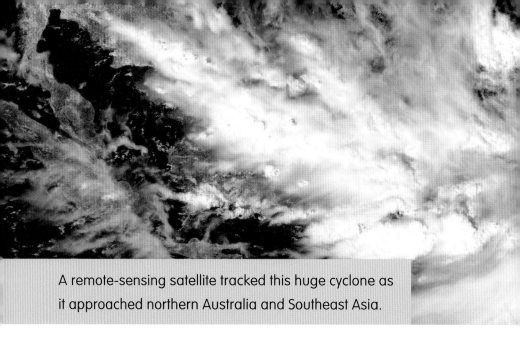

A remote-sensing satellite tracked this huge cyclone as it approached northern Australia and Southeast Asia.

Weather satellites

Many satellites collect information about and take photographs of Earth. They use **remote sensing**, which can detect and monitor the physical characteristics of an area. Special cameras in these satellites take images of large areas of the earth's surface, which allow us to see much more than we can see from the ground.

These satellites are used for forecasting the weather. The images they take show us cloud formations, rainstorms, dust storms and cyclones. Satellites provide vital information to governments so they can issue evacuation orders to people. Predicting dangerous weather events can help save lives.

Australian bushfires

This is a satellite view of bushfires in southern and eastern Australia. Images from satellites helped firefighters and water-bombing planes target areas to help put out the fires. The photos also helped authorities issue evacuation orders to residents.

When natural disasters strike, satellites can reveal bushfires and volcanoes erupting. They can also show damage from flooding, earthquakes and tsunamis. This can help emergency services determine where they are most in need and deliver aid more effectively.

Space archaeology

Can satellite images help us discover the past?

Archaeologist Dr Sarah Parcak says yes! She has found many previously undiscovered ancient sites, including the ruin of an ancient Egyptian city, by looking at satellite images of the earth's surface.

Archaeologists had been searching for this city for decades, but they could not find it. Then Sarah looked at photos taken from space using cameras that can show underground objects. She could clearly see the outlines of where buildings had once stood – she had discovered the lost city.

A satellite image of Cairo and the Nile River delta, Egypt

The ruins of Tanis, Egypt. Sarah Parcak used satellite imagery to uncover the city grid of Tanis.

From there, the discoveries rapidly increased. She found 70 sites in three weeks. It would have taken archaeologists three years to cover the same ground on foot. Sarah believes that less than 1 per cent of ancient Egypt has been discovered so far.

Satellites can take photos of almost every centimetre of land on Earth. Sarah realised that using satellite photos to discover ancient sites could open the door for millions of people around the world to become space archaeologists.

She has created an enormous online science project for kids and adults everywhere. Users can log into a **database** and view millions of images of Earth to identify possible archaeological sites.

People think I'm Harry Potter, and I wave a wand over an image and something appears and it looks easy . . . Any discovery in remote sensing rests on hundreds of hours of deep, deep study. Before looking at satellite imagery of a cemetery or a pyramid field, you have to already understand why something should be there.

Dr Sarah Parcak, Archaeologist, globalxplorer.org

Machu Picchu, Peru, is the famous lost city of the Incas. Sarah is using new satellite technology to map Peru so she and her team can uncover new archaeological sites.

25

Chapter 4

Mission to Mars

The first moon landing was 50 years ago. Today, there is a new goal – to land on Mars. In our **solar system**, Mars is the planet that is most like Earth. But it is hard to imagine we could ever live there.

What is the environment like on Mars?

Mars has half the sunlight we get on Earth, but higher levels of harmful ultraviolet rays. Also, the air is unbreathable, the temperature is like the Antarctic in winter and the soil is toxic to humans.

If humans were to colonise Mars, they would need a constant supply of fuel, water, food and oxygen. Most important is the need for water, because without water there can be no life.

How long would it take to travel from Earth to Mars?

No one knows for sure, but scientists estimate it could take anywhere between 150 and 300 days. It takes three days for a spacecraft to travel from Earth to the moon. A spacecraft mission to Mars would need to carry a lot of fuel and oxygen to get there and back, and to help humans live and work.

Mars is called the Red Planet.

Is there water on Mars?

Scientists have long known that Mars had polar ice caps like Earth, but they thought the ice had disappeared. Orbiting space probes with special radars have recently revealed that the ice is still there, but covered with layers of sand, which has protected the ice caps from melting. This exciting new discovery means that the red planet has water and, in theory, Mars can support life.

Has the challenge of travelling to Mars created new technologies?

Scientists are experimenting to create energy and fuels from renewable and available sources. They have found a way of splitting water using electricity so that there is an energy part and an oxygen part. This exciting technology would allow water to be used for both fuel and for breathing on Mars. It could also be used on Earth to help us reduce our use of fossil fuels.

Did you know?

In 2004, two robotic space vehicles called Mars Rovers landed on Mars to explore the surface of the planet. Originally, their batteries were meant to last for only 90 days, but they continued sending back valuable information for more than 14 years.

Craters on the surface of Mars

Could we grow food on Mars?

Growing food in space is another challenge for scientists. Researchers at NASA believe that if we did colonise Mars, astronauts would spend most of their waking hours just tending to crops so they could eat.

To make farming on Mars more efficient, scientists have invented leaf **sensors**. The sensor allows a thirsty plant to send a text message to say it needs more water. This would reduce the waste of water and of astronauts' time.

Farmers on Earth also benefit from this technology, which has been shown to reduce water use on crops by up to 50 per cent.

Conclusion

In the past 70 years, scientists have learnt many things about the planets in our **solar system** and space. But, most importantly, learning about space has helped us better understand our own planet. The technologies developed for space missions have had enormous benefit for us on Earth and will continue to as we keep exploring the universe.

> **We set sail on this new sea because there is new knowledge to be gained, and new rights to be won, and they must be won and used for the progress of all people.**
>
> John F. Kennedy, 1962

Glossary

antennae a pair of wires for sending and receiving signals

archaeologist someone who studies history through the remains and objects of ancient people

database a set of information organised on a computer

navigators people who plan how to get to a place

remote sensing collecting information without making physical contact, usually via satellite

satellite an object that moves around a planet *or* a machine that is sent into space

satellite dish a bowl-shaped antenna that usually receives TV signals

sensors devices that detect a physical property and react to it in a particular way

solar system our sun and the planets that move around it

Index